Liz and Tad

by Sean Sanders
illustrated by Ellen Joy Sasaki

Decodable 10

McGraw Hill Education

Bothell, WA • Chicago, IL • Columbus, OH • New York, NY

MHEonline.com

McGraw-Hill Education

Send all inquiries to:
McGraw-Hill Education
8787 Orion Place
Columbus, OH 43240

ISBN: 978-0-02-145785-4
MHID: 0-02-145785-9

Printed in China

9 10 11 12 13 DSS 28 27 26 25 24

Liz and Tad nap.

All the cats run!

Liz zigs and Tad zags.

Can the cats tag Liz and Tad?

Liz and Tad run in the mud!

All the cats zip in.

Fun!